T0149395

THE BACKGROUND CHECK
OR REASONS
FOR LIVING

FOUCHARD DECOSSARD

THE BACKGROUND CHECK OR REASONS FOR LIVING

iUniverse books may be ordered through booksellers or by contacting:

iUniverse
1663 Liberty Drive
Bloomington, IN 47403
www.iuniverse.com
1-800-Authors (1-800-288-4677)

ISBN: 978-1-5320-8914-5 (sc)
ISBN: 978-1-5320-8915-2 (e)

Print information available on the last page.

iUniverse rev. date: 11/18/2019

Contents

Faith, at the age of reason, is commonly the best way to convince and to educate. Friendship still stays the best reason to behave and Family, the best way to hope and to struggle. Above all, community of faith leads us to share and to promote life and social values. Society never really understands the link between faith and life where suicide is a common fact who destroys and keep people from trusting to others in many difficult ways. Many steps to reach to set the real importance of faith in todays life as threat to suicide is a strong link between deviance and delinquency in society.

The background check result is a factor of a future well being and a real attachment to life as community of faith promotes it. As it is, society gains in education of children and in freedom of religion to strengthen adults and young toward internal liberty and love of life. Society has to introduce religion in education whether or not family or parents could neglect

it. The simple fact of talking about human origin leads to pray and to meditate. The beliefs construct man's mind and strengthen it to achieve the goal which he was born for. Human kind needs to perceive, and to perceive, he needs to understand and to understand he needs to believe and to believe he needs an hero, a model, he needs God and Religion to bring him back where he was on that day when, troubling and despaired he tried to kill himself and to give up.

The simple fact that we know someone is watching us in every step of the life is a reason to watch one another and to be careful about what could be resulted in the next action. Faith relates human and life and community and promote social values as it improves social behaviors. Faith in a living community is a real support for society and advocates for human rights. Faith creates an other society inside and enlighten life, responsibilities of others. The fear of tomorrow in terms of previsions and uncertain actions are throwing away by the fact of a common take over. Faith, is a factor important to built a community and to grow

up. Faith based community is a miracle, goes beyond the simple fact of gathering together and let us praise the almighty and eternal Father. Faith based community is a reason for living: Prayers, weekly Gathering, meals, life, Wedding, baptism, friendship, respect and hope.

The simple fact that we know someone loves us is a reason to pay attention to tomorrow. Someone is waiting for us and we do not have the right to despair and to deceive him. Friendship help us handle unexpected situations and shapes us as we always have something to share one another. By building social relations with humans we construct our own personality and we get day after day some more reasons to live. Most thinkers, like sociologist relate your personality to whom you are connected with and perceive life as a response to the environmental (Sitz im leben). The interaction constructs life and pushes you to handle all obstacles you face. It is very important to relate your friends to a kind of hope inside a faith based community, in order to assure the necessary link between Faith and Friendship without this it is impossible to talk about. Because, life, in a relation, is the main

goal we are pursuing. If friendship is poor in spirit, it could become obstacle to make progress and can destroy the former objectives you had gained.

Be careful about what you can built in friendship if you cannot do it forever. Every step is to be supervised to know really to whom you are in relation, even for a simple friend like a classmate or someone else. Because you are looking for something which will last, and better forever. Your whole life depends on what you have done and how you have done it. Friendship is a choice in society, it is not a gift, it has not given to you like, brother, sister, mother, father. You choose your friends, you choose your spouse, building deep, durable relationship and strong family between (Man-Woman) or (Woman-Man) and a better knowledge about them will help you surely. Friendship inside faith based community constructs strong mental health and helps you reach real objectives in whole life.

1

Mental health and Real Objectives.

Mental health and rational thinking get along in life and let us pursue the real goal and realize the dream of your life. Mental health is a real fight as life become more and more difficult in Challenges, obstacles and finance. We will articulate the End and the beginning to achieve the common objective of the society. IT is not different from physical health, but a part of the whole structure, to built day by day. Mental health is a strong link between you and the environment about what support you received, and what response you gave. This is the first step to set a real goal and to be able to pursue it in real life, supporting by your environment like family, friends, teachers,. The whole society is building on the social mental health, because every human that acts gives his better performance in the living

environment. The result is that all institutions reach their goal and perform on time their duty. Everyone knows the real importance of mental health in a society when the task requires a kind of common sense to gather all who are involved day after day. It is like a social control in acting, to avoid deviance, delinquency, suicide and crime. It lets you improve your social behaviors, promotes life and leads you to long life careers.

The true objectives of your dream find their realization as you keep fighting and building strong social relations to each other in the workplace, in College or in any social structure. You are connected with a clear and specific goal for tomorrow according to the things you are dealing with. Most of the people engaged in College perceive a true objective and conceive in their own way what to be done in every step of the time to complete the process. Strong mental health is a common structure to built a better tomorrow because every where you will need it to perform and succeed. Educated people with strong professionals goals with better achievements, solve most issues (problems) of

life. When avoiding risky behaviors, by adopting healthy behaviors, we construct ourselves and our community. Mental health, rational thinking and practical actions interfere where life is a common objective to be kept instantly and to be protected. Faith-based community with a social good communication help you watch and understand the real importance of life and how to protect it by adopting a strong healthy behavior at all time.

Mental health and critical thinking let you set the link between the real objective or the professionals goals and the work place or the market to determine in a short or mid-term how related are the final goal and the realty. Because, Finance in the last step is to be calculated to weigh the economical cost of the objectives according to the workplace. It increases the work production and build the future by enhancing the career. Mental health is the health of a society. Some scholars tried to study how to strengthen human health by some psychological studies. They had concluded that sleep deprivation could affect mental health. The way society evolves depend on the spirit

which leads action and directs people mind. Lawmakers and leaders need to be in good health to handle obstacles and face life as they are conducting people toward their destiny. Mental health and critical thinking lead to practical actions which develop society and realize common aspiration. The perception of a good idea that constructs life and citizen aspiration is related to a psychological mind strongly attached to the benefit of a majority. Here mental health and rational thinking are related to built society as human stop thinking for himself but for the whole society. Community organizing belongs to those who believe that common aspiration is an important option and obliges everyone to decline selfish action and integrate social structure where followers and leaders share together the common task. Mental and physical health are so important that we need to improve health professionals life. (Like Physicians, Doctors, priests, pastors, social workers and so one). Good mental health help you fight against suicide. Early in your life you have to choose your friends and select your growth environment to prevent loneliness. Suicide is a result of bad mental health and a

lack of obligation. You need to care your loves ones as parents, spouse, and kids to evacuate at the right time any bad idea about threat to suicide. Because suicide is an act of betrayal against the family, friends and community. You need to appreciate life to understand what is going to be in the next day. Life is an obligation, it relates the fact to be realized even in difficult situations. Human has to work hard to keep him safe and healthy. The love of the others like family, parents, friends and community construct the obligation of life. Some times those connections (like family, spouse, friends,...) failed to keep you alive and can hurt you and make you unhappy, but you still have to believe in God and in life. Faith based community is the last place to protect you and, even you are abandoned you still have to believe and to fight against the evil that can appears in many others faces. You do not have the choice to give up, you must live and create the miracle for many others generations.

In some elementary and High schools, teachers used to enquire about what most of the students would like to study as professionals goals. And

the result was spectacularly evident that the large numbers of students would like to be physicians or Doctors or nurses for getting a better range of salary and have a good standing in society.

It is like a way to apprehend in the present time the future and to set the rules who command the achievement of those professionals goals. Society and young children gain by the time they start making a commitment for a future well being. Society, as it is fighting for the development of good characters, support ideas who lead to the accomplishment of those goals. Adult, youth and Society are related and watch each other to perform any individuals tasks and duty in this field. Good Mental health and rational thinking lead to practical actions in society as it evolves with the idea that strong and real objectives need healthy people. The whole society expect, in a short term some signs which reveal the hope of a better tomorrow. And any individual who fights for a good standing in society make a connection between the present and the future as Society still urges you to perform right now.

Real objectives are the strong ideas of your life which pushing you toward real action to prove what will be in the next step. Because in a developed country, where society keep trying to reconcile us by giving us what we need to success, we cannot stop fighting for a better life and make the necessary changes for the futures generations.

Those objectives are possible as society let them grow and strengthen them. A multiple way to achieve the ideas supporting by Society in many field (Grant, scholarship, Loan, and so far…). Everyone need to be connected to a social structure in order to improve day by day those positive ideas (like Church, faith-based community, community organizing, strong family, schools ….). As those structures support society to accomplish the daily task which leads to set and to perform the dream of all, they support also any individuals objectives in a good manner. Real objectives need to be supported and start making a link to the social contract that bonds individuals together. Real objectives help you pay attention in the present and set the rules to achieve them

necessarily. Real objectives help you shape your characters to avoid any misconduct which could dispel your effort to fight the good fight and to win. Background check is a result of the effort to achieve the dream of your life as Society promotes it. Community organizing and faith based community work together to enable youth to perform real objectives and improves life of elder people. They teach us to be responsible and to act like we do for the large number of people.

If connected to social structures, human's mind starts to think for the entire society and support ideas which lead to Global realization where everyone find its own goal and objective. Because, good mental health is a component of Love, pardon and understanding in family, society, Church and friendship ; real objective is a fight even those conditions are not established. Good mental health is a gift supported by the love of yourself, God and other. Mental health is a fight against any piece of darkness of any social structure which tried to erase you and forbid all your efforts to win. The gift of life soon supported by the

social structures is to be kept and used when, far away any other structure will try to fool you around. A response is important to life and to society as a contribution to life as society is getting old and needs to be renewed. Now it is time to give back what you received long time ago..

At the time you reach your forty years old, you are the one who help society get his speed by helping and criticizing it positively. You are student and master or teacher at the same time. Society is the gathering of individuals and you are one of them, you have to contribute to keep and to go beyond. At this time, you will support society efforts by your work for a better tomorrow. Mental health needs to be supported by environment but you have to fight against darkness to promote light and to achieve the dream of your life. It is a gift, and if it is a gift, it is to be conquered. If it is to be conquered, you have to fight against the evil and all obstacles that life brought related to collateral damages. And you cannot really win and achieve your goal without a good mental and physical health. Health to

perceive and to dispel the wrong, health and vision to select the way, health to understand human kind in his dialogue and relation to others. Ability to find what society brought as light and darkness, as good and Bad in the community to be organized. You cannot really win if you do not have what it takes to be done: Knowledge and Rational Thinking.

Education is a social contract based on both human nature and culture in society. It grows with your ability to keep instructions and to communicate. At the end, knowledge is the result of some instructions stored, and useful in many occasions. Knowledge supports your ability to think and perform your rational thinking. In most of the subjects you will need to be counseled to think rationally not emotionally. Without knowledge you will not be able to think rationally and it is important to weigh every step of your background check to relate action to thought. Some thinkers had tried to select ideas most common between scholars and to expand them as knowledge is also to be renewed and to be balanced. Action results and experiences are the most methods

to check link between knowledge and reality. And rational thinking is to be referred to realty to verified knowledge and set its own power. Community organizing ask for action, and practical actions to be a voice of people and to reflect to others young communities.

Education is an important step in any effort to realize real objectives and goals of your life. It enables your rational thinking and push you to criticize the way that knowledge is still transmitted to further generations. To act rationally, community needs proper knowledge at the right time. Education and community are related as Family and Society. Schools still keeps the light where knowledge is communicated, but community had tried to separate or to split knowledge as education and instructions.

Education belongs to family, church and environment and Instructions belonged to schools. Now we use for both Education as instruction become in result Education. Rational thinking based on instruction and education produce action in community organizing. But

it is a fact that human being make mistakes or sometimes act emotionally to satisfy his own power or ideas. At all times, community needs practical and rational actions to avoid delays and to dispel mistakes. Professionals goals are the duty of people whom nourish ideas in this field where community started and needed to be renewed. Real objectives and professionals goals to be achieved are the common task of leaders and future leaders of communities. Leaders have to act rationally and to act rationally, they need education and/or instructions. Faith based communities and communities organizing are the most common reasons for living and for fighting or struggling. Education is different from a place to another but, some individuals had passed away with a lack of education because the main is the love of your common native place: The love of your country to set the action which will permit future generations to live in peace and to bless you all time as they had really found a Legacy and lived with dignity.

The whole society, in some developed countries had tried to implement education and the

challenge is different from undeveloped countries where it is hard to reconcile people and to split the cake as some social services never worked nor satisfied population. In that place the common good is not shared and public safety has had duty to put an end to manifestation and to strike. The social contract had never existed and if, it has been abandoned to set other proper selfish actions. Those developed countries have not a lot to do in community organizing as population had received the services life required to start the social contract and to dream the society of tomorrow. Even Education is a long life process, it starts early in life and expands in professionals goals. And after, it realizes the daily task of a student that life instructs through friends, peers, members of society, church, family and so one. If the country is poor in resources, all citizen are poor. Some can be very rich but the result is always the same, it reflects a low level of education, lack of health insurance and low income. Education to be helpful has to integrate nationalism, citizenship, civism and love of the common legacy or love of the country. If some institutions failed to instruct

about civism and citizenship, Religion has always related Faith and communities and suggested real attachment to society, as the common living place.

2

Faith-based Community.

We had discovered together that the best place to enrich your brain is to evolve with a faith based community where love and forgiveness are shared. The brain runs the mental health, and human being has to know that he will have to fight to keep alive any piece of spirit he received since his birth. Faith based community is a living place above all and as it relates you to God it goes beyond society, and, if anyone who took part or if the leader really knows what it matters. It is a bond between earth and sky in what citizen failed to do, in what people could not understand, in what population fears to realize. Religion and/or faith based community is a nation who supports another one or a nation inside another one. The values and social norms are practical actions inside faith based communities and society recalls at the time of renewal the proper actions realized inside those communities to perform common

social duties. The teaching wish to recall social norms and push you to perform them. Inside those communities, life is not only a gift but also a task like a mission to accomplish. Faith-based community is a social contract called religion and related between believers. But a nation evolves quickly with community organizing and faith based community. Those communities support strong developmental ideas and create peace in society.

Law enforcement agents have to work closely with those communities because they are pursuing visible actions which promote peace and facilitate life for the elderly people. Religion has it as a record to be the one who had promoted life and social norms as an obligation to set the social contract. Social norms and morals characters has evolved to become a part of religious teachings. And some where, morals values in Religion went beyond society to criticize what it needs to perform the duty of the majority and to call back toward a renewal and improvements. Human being requires time to forge tomorrow and he had tried long time ago to achieve and realize his dream

to fight against death, sickness, misfortune. Even religion had brought some answers but many others questions still stayed unanswered. Community organizing is a response to life where suicide and misfortune had tried to cease any action to facilitate life and to put an end to fear and treason. By the way any individual who had collected ideas about community organizing had before worked to reconcile himself with the social norms and values. And so the background check is a result of an early engagement in life to set the rules and ideas shared by the majority. Because faith based communities and community organizing are strongly some reasons for living.

Without those reasons, life is like a confined space, closed and any action who could lead to save you can latterly betray you. Because life had never been an individual gift but something to share and to expand. Those communities are in the life long process the place where the real objectives and professionals goals become true. Adult and young support any effort to reconcile society and population through the achievement of true professionals

goals. And those tasks strengthen you to be true leader in a community and enable you to start early in your life the process to recall constantly the social contract and to succeed the background check as a daily duty. Faith based community is different from community organizing as it promotes faith and respect for religious values and social norms. Even when community organizing got a higher degree in formatting political ideas and facilitate local leadership movement, faith based community had reached an internal work for developing mind and spiritual growth of human beings. An everlasting work of human in the field of sociology who betrays a lack of education when supporting political ideas, some thinkers wished to evacuate religion and faith based communities. As the faithful is a part of the society and act for the common well-being we can't admit any idea which deny his citizenship and his political statut. Faith based community can insert community organizing.

It is not necessary to store a chapter for this matter as we try to solve it when community organizing evolves aside faith based

community. It integrates the same objectives as a community organizing not at all time but strongly cooperates at a high-level to anticipate lay leadership program and to convince people about the interest to share those goals and to vote. In fact some communities organizing had not reached such a political extension but still tried to solve local issues and claimed the potential values of their community to be shared by state leaders and to raise funds by selecting some important credentials. Although some communities organizing stay in a low level of political movement, it is the sum of a big movement when adding all communities who had supported some leaders to run the presidential campaign and to succeed. Community organizing integrates social and political life and support individuals goals as those individuals wished to solve local issues and participate in social life. And the real objectives are response to societal gift and effort to achieve the dream of the community. Community organizing acts fast and does not need to wait for political movement to start making the necessary changes. When those communities insert political ideas, they could

loose their credibility and stop acting as local movement or local organization if any political party tried to integrate them. Because they must gather any individual who share the community's life or anyone who lives in this community has the right to take part.

Those ideas developed by communities led to practical actions and selected individuals with strong mental health to pursue the dream and to solve further issues. Some individuals evolved with community organizing and had had strong ideas to anticipate about what could be the next action to keep safe and alive the community. Those issues construct early in life the mind and spirit of some individuals who are involved in solving problems and social issues. Sometimes they anticipate local leaders and propose the necessary change in advance. Their brain work hard to be at all time on duty and to perform. Practical actions and rational thinking are the common duties of local leaders to give an adequate response to social issues and to bring solutions to societal problems.

Critical thinking and community organizing work together to prioritize ideas in a short-term or mid-term goals by selecting some important challenges whose credentials require a quick action. Local leaders need to understand at the present time which issues must be solved and prioritize ideas to lead actions. Some ideas appear and disappear, but professionals leaders will have to be instructed about the result by practicing shortly some ideas connected with the problems to be solved. Now we understand the necessary link between leaders and real objectives or professionals goals to be achieved in the field of community organizing. because we cannot expect any other thing better with a low level of Education and a lack of civism. Ideas emerge and die as phenix, because ideas must be linked or connected to the community expectations to be selected. Critical thinking helps you prioritize issues to be solved and let you select strong ideas which lead to practical actions and everlasting or durable solutions. Community organizing is a little bite different from faith based community because it has to select his leaders as the challenges became more and more exciting.

Because of the individuals who took part in the community had already reached their professionals goals, community organizing has a multiple field to investigate and collect issues and ideas quickly to involve local leaders in planning meeting. By selecting and prioritizing the credentials to convince people and to find necessary funds to act, local leaders had realized the most important part of their duty. Community organizing constructs society and builds a new world for the future generations. Practical actions need more power to inventory the field or the extent of communities expectations in a short-term realization which betray some handicaps when trying to set the first action, finance delays. Community organizing and local organizations need their own financial source and have to collect funds from local members regularly. Members have to work and contribute. Some kind of peace from a regular budget executed every day to set the family expenses well balanced about what you earn and what you spend. Community is like a family to balance budget every day. And individuals who take part in communities contribute in both family and community.

Work and finance are important parts of life, we can't succeed without finance to give on time a response to the needs of family. Good mental health requires strong ideas about the link between money- or finance- work and familial expenses. Methods to face life and to set the social contract start with the ideas that human beings have to work to support his family. When those conditions are available like physical health, community organizing and family become more and more powerful.

Work and Finance in community are the straight line toward people had stepped even when some still had been looking for finance before work. But it is a common destination toward individuals and professionals had tried to practice their knowledge and to succeed. Work is different from finance even if they have had the same source. To get finance, you have to work. And you can build your economical power from investment, you can be rich and never work hard cause of a legacy. Because your parents or grand-parents had worked very hard you inherited enough funds to support your family. But you still have to work because work

is not only to receive salary, money or finance, it is an investment, your own contribution to build the community and to achieve the goals long time ago that your grand parents had implemented. It is the common duty of citizen and habitants in a country where peace and respect had been settled as basic rules to promote life. The hard and regular work of citizen strengthen the social contract, built the community and expand freedom and liberty. Work had been doing to achieve society which is a constant in the equation W=S., stopped deviance, delinquency and crime: Work= salary. Work is an obligation to perform your own personality and to raise in a higher degree your potentials. You ignore you, you ignore what you are able to if you never try.

Work is balanced with restless time to evaluate yourself, to strengthen your body and to renew your energy, to pray, to meditate and to work better. Work=Salary is a rule in the work code, rights of employee, but sometimes your work worth more than your salary. And the result is when choosing your professionals goals you have to pick a love one in order to give a

better performance in the workplace. By your work, you build your community, you evaluate yourself and you take care of your family. It is like an adaptation to your environment and a certain way to be attached to life. IT helps you find the equation which solves the main issues of your life if you are very smart to calculate accurately Salary, expenses, savings and perhaps investment. Your work had saved you and let you achieve your goals, because you cannot live in dignity without the money you received from your work. It is not a gift it is an obligation to get payed.

Finance in a community is an obligation to support your own family and to provide to loves one the necessary goods to live in dignity. Some individuals need to be educated about the impact of finance in human life. Bankruptcy leads to suicide and it requires early in life to process the better way to manage money by balancing budget and salary and to solve accurately financial issues. Savings money and balancing expenses are the best way to fight bankruptcy and to announce latterly some ability to invest with truthful and credible

friends or investors. Social workers have to counsel people about what could result if anyone cannot balance his budget. He failed to respond to his obligation and cease his contract to his client. Work and finance fit you to face life and to live with confidence by realizing your dream. Financial resources have to be used with planification and your whole life depends on what could result if bankruptcy pushed you to give up or to abandon. People needs to be careful about finance and the spiritual growth. Faith based community, even when money do not have the biggest importance, has to rely the spiritual growth to resources available for the entire community like it appears in the beginning in the first Christian communities. The Apostles had shared together all their goods. Finance is an important part of your life, work finances your budget. W-F-B. The connection between those concepts and ideas, in practical actions make the necessary change of your life and prepare you to solve accurately local organizations problems and respond to communities expectations.

Faith based community and community organizing had reached a new concept in the field of anthropology as human can not be separated. This concept leads researchers to understand the extending of the domain knowledgeable and realized that all aspect of human life need to be conceptualized and underlined (Jesus feeds people who were listening to his Word as the night approached. Jn 6).. The present needs to be seized on time and the whole human life requires all the importance it appears to attach to the study in this matter. Those communities, by this global conception kept their leadership in a long life process and stopped any doubt about the result of a lack of ability to solve social issues. They had started to connect all human life elements in a developed country where everyone has to produce and to produce on time the goods he needs to forge his own personal power and to participate to the social structures. And so the result is what occurred in the last decades where some communities had been involved in political party to contribute to make the necessary change in society. Because of a lack of necessary goods can contribute to

lessen communities life and /or to make them disappeared.

Community organizing and local organizations early understood their impact in society as they kept trying to raise local problems and to solve them. Members had fought to lessen issues and to improve human life. Community organizing supports society in its fight to make itself a better place for human development. Faith based community and community organizing switched together in the sociological field to improve human life in society. WE can connect now the necessary link between: Health-Faith-Work and Finance where solid and true professionals goals stand accurately.

3

Professionals Goals
and the workplace.

Some students have had many difficulties to choose their professionals goals because they need to inventory the positions available in the workplace and to set the rules to succeed when achievements are related to the needs of the society. Most of the students selected some positions where salary are higher than ever and some others tried to pick the most valuables professions in the society: like Physician, nurse, lawyers, Business and so one …. But, you need to know what you expect from life to choose a field of study and /or you have to love some professionals goals to be all life long engaged to respond accurately to the needs of your partners or clients. In both directions, performance is an obligation, and professionalism a duty. Most of the young choose the profession they like without trying to look for a better one

according to the salary, the prestige and the characters that have been affected in the past to raise the issue of a common fight across many generations to reach a certain notoriety. This is the best way to solve some careers issues when choosing a professionals goals according to your inclination and to your ability. You early solved some academicals problems and evacuate misfortune, stress and sadness in the workplace.

Students need to be supported by individuals, bank, local authorities, government and family to reach their goals. Community organizing interfers to support his own individuals sometimes and government grant finance in a large part the study of many students. Finance is important in seeking professionals goals and the support you could find help you reach your goal. It matters whether or not if at the end you will be able to pay back the loan you received for your studies. This is the problems of many students, when approaching professionals goals because they are not able to finance they keep tracking the most valuable fields of study, the higher degree of studies to reach quickly

the workplace and to pay back the loan. We have to raise the issue of diversity as the large numbers of students could be forced to track goals emotionally. It is accurate that some true expectations had still kept this matter as an unsolved problem for the middle class which had tried to delay the loan payment and lessen interest. The doubt about choosing professionals goals after high school graduation had long time ago pushed students toward two most valuable and accountable fields:

A)- Health professionals goals.
B)- Administration.

Health professionals goals could become: Physician, nurse, Pharmacist, Radiologist, assistant. After graduation, students or former students became professionals and tried to reach the workplace by selecting institutions where the salary is the best to provide the necessary funds to pay back the loan and to start saving according to some specific objectives. Medical studies are considered as the most expensive but, in United States physician and doctors, nurses are always asked and professionals

in this field will not have to wait for to find employment.

Administration is a common part of any institution which tries to survive and to answer to the needs of the clients. All institutions solicited an administrator to share with the technicians, the proper employees of an institution, the task to anticipate risk and to evacuate accurately delay in stock, production/ produce and to facilitate the whole duty to satisfy the community. When studying administration, according to the needs, it could be split in Hospital management, business Administration, school administration and perhaps enterprise management, Factory. You will only, require some class or some specific documentations to seize the domain of your further actions. Although those domains had elected their proper field of application and true methods, like schools. The technicity belongs to teachers, principal and assistant who are strongly prepared in Education. Administrator will have to manage finance and human resources as he keeps watching everyone to perform the proper task.

Those professionals goals are set to facilitate the work of the majority involved in Education and in formatting ideas to enhance and to enrich the domain of applicable goals. And even some of them are not straightly set in a proper field, students will have less issues to solve when trying to choose their own profession. And shifting from an emotional concept in selecting professionals goals, we have reached together the most valuable interest when students and young tried to connect society and profession ;it is not a given method but, those students will have to check and balance when adopting ideas to engage their future. Society is not the protagonist but it keeps tracking students and push them to solve and to care in their choice the most societal expectations. Students will have to select in this matter when and where they will have to implement and invest to satisfy the societal needs as they had received an unpredictable understanding of their problems like: (Scholarship, grant, College credit,… and so one).

Professional goal is an inner concept, susceptible to format individual personality. It

solves in advance some mental issue as it is a choice, an internal choice to face and to adjust life according to the needs of individuals and society. It keeps fighting to engage freedom and liberty as a right to practice true profession and solicit a large number of values to model and protect professionals duties. It is a freedom's space not to be conquered because life depends on (it). When acting, it is an human extension, and profession forges cultural concept to fight against savage nurture. It integrates human life, shape it and announces future well-being. The choice needs to be clarified and selected as life become more and more difficult.

Sometimes the door are largely open in some domains to encourage good characters and to create careers. Social workers expertise the domain of interest to evaluate the extent of solid attach which could explain some expectations. Now goals are not stressful to force choice into a specific domain because students will not have to pay back the scholarship. They are more confortable and approach professionals goals as a gain and an advantage. Students work hard to merit what life offers and keep studying to

realize their dream. Professionals goals are duty to accomplish in a delay acceptable according to parents expectations. It has been considered as an important step in life to start working and to give back to community what you should receive. Unfortunately some students had not been efficiently supported to produce the necessary change of their life. They kept their high school diploma as a gift and tried hard to push their kids into unprecedent domains. Everyone will have to create his proper domain of investigation to act in society and to advocate the human rights where a lack of personalized services could affect elders life and weaken social contract. Leaders in community organizing make the choice to fight all times against handicaps and solicit help from members to facilitate social life. By getting a good profession, individuals involved in community organizing could raise funds to perform and achieve their own accession to community leadership.

Professionals goals and the workplace contribute to fund you by practicing your profession and selecting strong methods to balance Budget

and salary as you tried to save money for further obligations as grant, aid and to finance local organizations. With great achievements in your life you become an important personality capable to finance local organizations and to promote true change in your community. Lay leadership and community organizing are the straight line to political influence and the beginning of real objectives. Lay leaders have to accomplish some professionals goals to stand. Community and local organizations support ideas to deal with local issues and start the process to select leaders and members to solve those problems. Solving and financing local organizations problems are strong reasons for living.

4

Solving problems.
Reasons for living.

Some thinkers had, at the beginning, asked this question: Is life worth living? Even life could not worth living, individuals need some reasons for living. It is like a mathematical problem to reduce to an equation the challenge of life. But some local leaders had not needed such a philosophical argument to answer quickly to those questions as life still was a daily perception and a daily battle to make it possible in solving unexpected problems and dealing with others more strongly attached to human nurture like deviance, delinquency and crime. Community organizing and faith based communities had answered to the cosmological argument when trying to solve societal problems as they belong to God and act to demonstrate the God's love for human beings. God exists and life worth living. Human being needs to be challenged

and it appears both happiness and sadness did not make the solid attach to life. You never know what leads to suicide. Most of the time, some misfortune tried to discourage you and to cancel the strong reasons of your life which led you to accomplish the dream of your family. Human being needs a reason to live, a strong reason. The strong reason is your own life, your personality, you at the present time: God and his Beloved son Jesus.

Faith based community had implemented its action to give a response to the belief that God wants a true change in every human being. So the actions of lay leaders wished to facilitate faith and to realized the dream for a social justice in the world through the community. Some local leaders had abandoned their own life to implement durable solutions for many social issues in communities like water, food, elementary school for children, health insurance and hospital. Some others had passed away with the ideas to reduce some issues related to poverty, justice and freedom and had, unfortunately, never realized the dream by putting an end to life with the regret to leave

those problems unsolved. Some reasons to live are the work of our teachers in school, the hard work of health professionals in hospital, the durable work of social workers, the work of every human being to build the community and to protect goods and life. Some more reasons to live are the true attach to family, friends and communities.

By solving problems, local leaders are called to worship and to celebrate life. Lay leaders are attached to communities life and tried to solve issues by raising sufficient necessary funds. A kind of true attachment to life early in childhood contribute to make a change in your life. All leaders have an history about what challenge they have already dispelled and evacuated to demonstrate their civism and their attachment to the community. As those members and leaders of local organizations had been fighting for getting more importance in their community, they had before worked for a better commitment to social contract and had realized the dream to comply or to satisfy the will of the society. By solving social issues, leaders and followers had recalled the basic rules

and integrated social norms as part of their life. Those choices in society set the background check as a constant recall to implement the common will and to announce some important change as part of those problems to be solved. Leadership requires an history and a true attachment to values and social norms who betray the background check as it evolves with the idea that local leaders had already solid attach to social norms to evacuate and solve problems rationally.

Community organizing act rationally and the background check is a part of community organizing and faith based community to implement actions and select local and lay leaders. Local leaders keep tracking their realizations as their own to propose to communities when they tried to get an higher degree in the community organizing or any other local organization. Some local leaders still adopt this method to evaluate their history as a background check. Leaders and followers have to work together ; ideas come from leaders and followers have to practice. Practical actions are not necessarily resulted from actions, local

leaders have to perform to be practical and to criticize the next action. From elementary school to College, students must be careful about their choice and their professionals goals to integrate life and to contribute to solve problems in communities. Practical actions are resulted from rational and critical thinking. Solving problems in faith-based communities are true reasons for living not for leaving.

Some families had worked hard to educate their children in some countries where education is not easy. But, they had been trying to achieve the most important actions of their life because they have loved those children and had struggled to facilitate life. Even when some true conditions had not been realized, they had kept tracking a good education for their kids. Community is not a lonely fact, it builds itself and any other positive action contribute to raise some societal problems and support ideas which will lead to construct the society. Community is the result of many positive actions. Sometimes, those families had never tasted the benefit of their hard work and died suddenly cause of stressful life and misfortune. But, they had

forged for others generations to believe in the miracle that life brings. Solving problems in communities requires good knowledge about society and if the past generations had tried to solve some social issues, more children could expect education at a higher level.

Community organizing contribute to support good ideas and to solve some true challenge in life. when trying to solve accurately those issues, families and community have had really some reasons to resist and to fight as those problems have still been tracking human life and reduced ability to act rationally. we cannot give up the true fight to live in a better place and human being has evolved with the idea that society needs to be renewed. In some place most of the work has to be done and because of a lack of resources it had been leaving to further generations. Many others situations had conducted human toward big realizations when they tried to help others or to fight problems in society. We will have to stop thinking for ourselves to watch the obligatory work which constantly recall our civism and our common sense of duty to be realized. It is

the reason for living which evacuates suddenly the deprivation and the threat of suicide and bring us back to life as it appears that someone or many others have not had the chance we got in life to struggle and to perform.

Selfish actions are not part of communities organizing but, if it produces positives actions it will be a part of societal construction as society is different from community organizing. Some individuals will have to integrate social contract as a part of their life to contribute to communities activities. A lack of challenges can destroy your ability to create and leads you to bad situation. And you will have to challenge you day after day to shake life and to shape you as it contributes to give a new sense to your goals and to stay motivated. Even some individuals worked separately to solve their own problems they will have to solicit local organizations expertise and to switch because community have always been a common place to gather any individual. Community organizing is an obligation in society, it provides goods for all and settle early the rules and shape individuals. It anticipates, when acting, to solve issues

and others problems raised in meeting whose credentials command short-term goals. Local leaders have had to daily deal with issues that have been raised in meeting and to solve them quickly and accurately because they were very shapes. Community organizing and faith based communities are win-win institutions to solve and anticipate solutions for the entire society and /or community. Individuals with strong professionals goals expect to lead local organization by adopting and studying good profession.

When James tried to go to College, he didn't know what profession to pick. As he was involved in local organization early in life, he has been thinking about providing to his community services in health management. And the idea to switch to medical studies came accurately. But, before he has never selected medical studies as an interesting field as his father was a teacher in elementary school. Some reasons or some good reasons pushed him to achieve the best thing in his life. After seven years balanced with some part time job and math lessons to kids in the neighborhood he

had picked the profession and was graduated. Some others reasons in life could at a certain time let you make it. Human being needs more reasons to challenge life. Those reasons have been advanced your birth and still exist. You need to perceive and to help up to find out when someone asks for help, when bad news become habits and children never stop crying.

When political leaders used societal problems to empower their political influence, local leaders act only to be a part of the society. In this matter we do not need to know the motivation, we only wish to evacuate issues and keep away from population some unsolved problems like sickness, lack of education, poverty by adopting durable solutions and install adequate institutions to manage new challenges and secure environment. Solving problems is the straight line toward local organizations and local leaders had stepped for the last decades. Those reasons anticipated some internal and personal reasons and produce unexpected achievements, unpredictable events and construct strong personality. Human being had never been the result of a selfish life, as he

promoted community he built a new world for him and for the entire society. He has always had a reason to live, to fight, to pray and to meditate. He has always had a family, a kid who never stops crying, a friend, a spouse, an elder to care and a community to watch and to support. And early in life he follows Jesus, keeps teaching and accomplishing social norms to reach and achieve his goals.

Those reasons enable you to act fast and to postpone your own life for biggest achievements. Some local leaders had been working all life long in community and had never stopped. They integrated communities as a part of their own life and has always stayed connected to new environmental goals to be realized. They had always set a goal to be achieved because community is a movement like a mobile human beings organization tracking at all time what could be the next action to anticipate and to promote life. This document would like to select some reasons to live and to announce life as a gift of God to be conquered and implemented. It tried to discover and to expand solid attachment to

life as an obligation. It rejects first of all the ideas to question life because human being can solve his environmental issue fully equipped with reason and ability to perform. The work that ancestors had been doing in hard climatic conditions are enough proof to fight the actual fight and this work needs to be achieved. You cannot give up.

Solving problems is a daily task and it requires finance. Local organizations and some professionals fight for resources to support actions. But, most of them ignore the better way to grow income and increase funds to support ideas and manage social issues. When collecting funds from members of organizations some local leaders had tried to increase those funds by investing. Professionals leaders have to know how to invest money to reduce deficit, and grow income. Investment is an obligation to succeed when managing local organizations because some issues ask for money to be solved and more money you have the better response you give to real challenges. Investment has its own rule and tactic. Some individuals invest without any good knowledge in this field. He

(they) will have to be supported by an other professional, You need to perceive the extent of your investment and it is important for you to try to invest in your own professional field even you will have to collect ideas from others peers. An other smart individuals had tried to study as they are investing to accurately respond to emergency and laziness from employees. You do not have the right to invest all your saving because investing is a risk and professionals wish better work than investing. Community organizing is a support for investment and local leaders solicit accommodation when investing required members to participate. The domain of your investment has to be completely manageable.

Solving problems requires a kind of future projection to anticipate action and to collect and save money to be ready in all time. It is a long life duty and local leaders or lay leaders had strong experience after decades and decades by selecting and prioritizing issues to be solved quickly and accurately. The human brain needs to be challenged and everywhere, even in the profession or in daily work; human being works

hard and get more and more experience when fighting to solve life problems and to give adequate response. As it is, the background check confirms the daily duty and the hard and rationally work that human has been doing to give birth to this community. Human being finds strong reasons to live and life is worth living.

Community leadership and socials workers had tried to counsel individuals about the extent of the importance of life in society. Born for another one, human being is a socius. He is an associate to someone else and he has to perform in faith and hope the duty affected to his competency. Mission is a new word to be explained. He has a mission whose constant attachment will reveal God's love for humanity. Some hazards in life are supported by the Creator and human being doesn't have the intelligence to understand the distance between life and death and effort to recuperate time in the daily battle between God and the Adversary. Time is a perpetual movement between death and life and human being must be strictly attached to his proper life condition to fight against the

evil and to accomplish his Mission. First, stay alive" without doing nothing" is already a fight. Because you can praise, you can worship and you can thank God. Second, working is another way to fight, but, here, you have to do GOOD work.. Now we, all, understand how human life is important to God to save humanity. God is the strongest reason for living.

Without the support of the community, individual does not have enough reasons to live and fail to respond to the Savior call. He could be present without acting, he could act negatively all time and he could die even he is still alive. Suicide is an option. And parents and communities have to work together to educate kids and children early in life to adopt social conditions leading to improve and to appreciate life. Those conditions are fully communicated in Faith-based communities and reflected in society. And when children are fully equipped with good instructions how life is shared and need to be expanded, suicide will never be an option. Those sad conditions have been solved already and life got a new sense. Parents, in this matter, will have to act quickly and facilitate

social structure to constantly recall the duty to live without fear and regret as individual will integrate social norms, respect and moral values. We will have to switch and balance characters as life is a common gift and so, to be living in community.

Happiness in life is resulted to the whole duty and your proper accommodation:. Good salary, well balanced life, friends, parents and family. But, all those things are to be kept. Happiness is fast, you must have your own reason to live and without some external conditions. Love is a reason to live and without accommodation. Faith introduces you to life and makes life possible even some conditions never exist, and fights death. Faith in community helps you create and anticipate future. Faith strengthens you for hard mission and equipped you to face life and to survive. Faith keeps the community alive and reflects other members to achieve their proper duty. Lay leaders are more accountable to Church than communities because faith build communities. Reason to live is not happiness, reason to live is attachment to life

in community and family. Happiness goes fast, community and family will last for ever.

Those mental issues are to be solved and lay leaders, Pastors have to work quickly to evacuate all doubt about the obligation to live and to promote life. Even local leaders tried to solve some problems in the community, some individuals still faced inner issues to be solved. Pastor and leaders have more to do than visible issues in communities. As human being is a constant part of the society we have to make sure of his accountability by helping him to reach the higher mental health to perform his proper task in society. Freedom and liberty are true expressions of sociological human condition to act and facilitate life as a part of the community to be promoted and developed. Local leaders strongly educated and instructed will have to raise solid attachment to life and to educate members about the obligation to stay connected to the morals values and social norms and to live even some true conditions are not realized: life is a gift of God. Suicide is against the law. Suicide must be punished.

It is the duty of the entire society to put an end to suicide by sentencing everyone who kill himself. Even after death, They must set the trial in absentia, pronounce the sentence. It will help us to deter suicide and to find out what have led individuals to suicide. We will discover those invisible creatures who had conducted human being to suicide and to seize them. Suicide has always been a call for more justice, a sign of internal sufferings inside the whole society, an invitation to criticize the criminal justice system. It had been formatted to fit the voice of invisible creatures to set and to make important changes in the society. Even when those domains still stayed unrevealed, the matter has to be underlined. Some of those cases could be personalized but, the threat needs to be evacuated and solved. A sociological analyze to set how the proper aspects of individuals life had been satisfied or not, to conduct some studies and to respond adequately in any effort of improvement of social structures.

These developed countries would not have to face such a specific problem as most of the

needs had been satisfied and the human rights have been long time ago advocated. An other problem to solve, unpredictable, unprecedented and invisible. This is the last, in its case.(sui generis) ; and we will start, early in life, to fight any aspect which will lead people to suicide. It reveals a lack of love for the country, for the structures, and a manifestation of an act of refusal to cooperate and to survive. It is an act of betrayal: You should have more reasons to stay alive.

It's time to stay connected. Time to fit local legislation to universal legislation. Time to inventory the divine law. Surely those unexpected situations question every human being about the probable cause of the decision of individual to put an end to his own life. Leaders and researchers have to work hard to strengthen some existing living structures and to enforce some domains affected to the health management system. They will have to review the Justice system and act quickly to make the necessaries changes. They will have to study every little case to raise issue unsolved and to relate it to the global structure. Because life is

worth living. Faith-based community has its own contribution to give to society to solve issue related to the social justice system. And in this domain, it remains hard to seize the potential threat that affects every citizen in the society. Because of this lack of knowledgeable object, it will be very difficult to solve it accurately. We need the good will of everyone to care of his own family and to pay attention to any piece of sadness or anxiety which could lead to suicide.

Local leaders, health professionals and social workers will have to work together to expand information, to educate and to support individuals efforts to facilitate life, like sports, organizations and meetings in order to strengthen life and to evacuate anxiety. Adulthood and youth will have to cooperate as they are moving among the place to warn local authorities about any potential case. Even it is an unpredictable situation, sometimes it could happen that some signs or symptom are visible. Like loneliness, sadness and remarkable absence. Family and friends will have to reinsert individuals in the community to make sure on what could be going on. Because all of us,

will have perhaps to be alone, to be sad or, everyone will have to face loneliness, or sadness and so one.

Not only local leaders, but everyone has to try to solve societal problems as he still is a part of the community. He will contribute in his proper manner to help law enforcement agents, local authorities, religious leaders about what could be a potential threat to peace in the city like: Racial profiling, discrimination against minority, crime, suicide. Solving problems has always been a strong reason to live among peers.

The country is ours, the state is our legacy, the city saves us, the town protected us and we have to live in peace by supporting any local effort to improve life. Our will to live in the city is our history and our reason to live. The background check is our history on what we did to make life possible and how it has been done. It is our love for the country which had fed us and kept us alive. It is our will to cooperate and to contribute to the development which will conduct us to advocate for human rights and to comply to social norms and morals values. This

love for the country had been pushing us to solve the most difficult problems that has been raised and bring durable solutions to others one. Even some problems still stayed unsolved like suicide and violent crime, health professionals and local leaders will have kept working hard to bring in a short -term some durable solutions and to cooperate to law enforcement agents in community organizing. The hard work of law enforcement agents and local leaders in solving social issues had given us true reasons to live and to hope.

This document has tried to increase the social link between community and individuals and set the question which had been for many centuries the purpose of most of the thinkers. Is life worth living?. Individuals, students and adults, by achieving some real professionals goals and solving local organizations problems and communities obstacles, by taking care of their own family had found enough reason to live, to fight and to detect, to deter and to prevent ultimately the threat of suicide. As they have wished to lead local organizations and communities, they have also fought to adopt

and integrate universal moral values and social norms. It sets, finally, that life has always been a gift to be conquered and to be realized in Faith-based communities by developing true attachment to God, to family, truthful and credible friends and society.

Early in life some important challenges empower you, as a citizen, as a leader and make you happy to read latterly your own history. The background check could be finally the history of a given life for the community or for the country in what you have done, in what you have failed to do.

V-Is it matter?

Something bad could happen in your life, but always start by tracking the straight line, the choice of the majority, the most reasonable to be successful. Be aware to do in all time the best choice and to produce. You don't have the right to waste your time, you don't have the right to waste your money. Production could be more than physical thing that you can evaluate. The peace to produce, the peace

in the city is the main area for the economical progress. Everyone must live in peace. You have to protect and to advocate the peace for the entire society. Health, work and finance contribute to peace. You won't have to blow your mind, you will get to install your peaceful life by balancing your expectations with your financial budget.

The Society supports everyone in life to reach and to realize better goals and to struggle to deal with the common aspiration and the majority expectations. You have the right to be educated and to know the Will of God in order to make the best choice. Find out what human can do and how. The Bible, the Church, the society and the family will help you to be in peace with God. Keep tracking the will of God through his Beloved Son, JESUS... When you feel weak, pray and you will find strength to continue on your way.

You must live in peace in a democratic country where civils liberties and civil rights are well protected. The well being of the society is the common duty of every one. Try soon in life

to escape yourself from dramatical issues by adopting faith in religion and let the darkness to others. Try to surround you of goods friends to avoid collateral damages. If elders stop sharing their old experience, even bad or good, future generations could not face life as it brings more challenges every day. Try early in life to set the rules of your contract and to integrate them. Human being is incomplete without God, he will need to deal with society expectations and to comply to social norms. Human life is the product of the work of the entire society. AS you manage your life, you manage society. Education and well doing are the keys. Better to know that, even late in life than to ignore it. You will make the biggest achievement in your whole life. Thanks God! The Lord is with you! Because you are looking for him, and you are waiting for his salvation as you still try to serve him in the universe.

I have competed well, I have finished my race, I have kept the faith. (Second Letter to TIMOTHY 4,7).

Printed in the United States
By Bookmasters